MOVING TO BALI
Living in Paradise is Easier Than You Think

©2024 JR Education Corp

Table of Contents

Introduction

Chapter 1: *Getting Legal* - Visas

Chapter 2: *Show Me the Money* – Banking & Taxes

Chapter 3: *Just What the Doctor Ordered* – Healthcare and Health Insurance

Chapter 4: *Some Light Housework* – Renting or Buying a Home in Bali

Chapter 5: *Dude, Where's My* ~~Car~~ *Motorbike?* – Buying a Motorbike and Getting a Driver License

Chapter 6: *Retail Therapy* – Shopping & Shipping

Chapter 7: *Are You Gonna Eat That?* – Food & Drink

Chapter 8: *The Honeymoon Is Over.* – Challenges to Living in Bali

Chapter 9: *Where to Now?* – Locations

Chapter 10: *Say What?* Survival Indonesian

INTRODUCTION

I've been going to Bali for over twenty years now. Every time I step off the plane, I fall more and more in love with this island. Bali has long been romanticized by Western travelers – from anthropologists like Margaret Mead and the Blaire brothers, to its status as a home to AWOL soldiers during the Vietnam War, to modern-day drug runners, Bali has both a rich and sordid history. Living in Bali is certainly not without its challenges – as this book will tell you. However, once you're drawn to the island and its incredible people, it's hard to imagine ever leaving. If you've visited Bali and are considering making it your new home, you know this feeling all too well. If you haven't visited this island paradise, then I hope this book inspires you to go a little further and get that plane ticket.

Some Facts on Bali and Indonesia

The Indonesian archipelago is the most populous country in Southeast Asia. It is made up of over 17,000 islands. More than half of Indonesia's population lives on Java (just north of Bali). The capital of Jakarta is situated in the northern part of Java – about a two-hour plane ride from Bali's Ngurah Rai airport. The official language of Indonesia is *Bahasa Indonesia* (or simply *Bahasa,* which means language). However, Bahasa Indonesia is a language of unity. As with many parts of the world where natural geographic borders exist, there is tremendous linguistic diversity. Over 580 languages or dialects are spoken throughout the country.[1] The people of Indonesia are as diverse as the languages and the landscape. While agriculture is predominant in many rural parts of Indonesia, Bali is highly dependent on tourism.

The currency of Indonesia is the rupiah (IDR). Indonesia is a developing nation, and its currency is often volatile. At the time of writing, the value of $1 USD is roughly 14,250 IDR. According to World Bank data, Indonesia reported total GDP of just over $1.05 trillion USD in 2020 – or approximately $3,870 GDP per capita.[2] While many Indonesians still struggle with poverty, the percentage of those living below the international poverty line has fallen dramatically since the 1990s. Life expectancy is also increasing.[3]

Along with the increasing income and life expectancy, Indonesia is experiencing growth in its adult literacy rate as well – which stands above 95%.[4] However, challenges surrounding education remain glaringly obvious. Despite this growth in adult literacy, the World Education News and Review indicates that Indonesia has one of the highest rates of *functional illiteracy* in Southeast Asia (functionally illiterate means students can read a text but are unable to answer questions about it).[5] Moreover, there is a great disparity in the education that is available to children in different parts of Indonesia. While Bali has some excellent international schools, most staffed with foreign-trained teachers, many of these schools come with a hefty price tag attached to them.

Bali also exhibits great religious tolerance and diversity. Indonesia is the most populous Muslim nation in the world. During the fasting month of Ramadhan, it is common to see restaurants closed from sunup to sundown. Those that do remain open often have curtains over the windows to respect those that are fasting. Bali is unique in that it is predominantly Hindu. Further, people travel from all over Indonesia to seek jobs in Bali's tourism industry. This results in more and more religious diversity on the island, with churches (both Catholic and Protestant), synagogues, and mosques alongside Bali's Hindu temples.

Situated in the tropics – between the islands of Java and Lombok, Bali is an island with a population of roughly 4.25 million. The population is largely concentrated in southern Bali, where the capital, Denpasar, is located. Since Bali has experienced such vigorous international growth over the last two decades, its population is spreading out from the southern tourist hotspots – like Kuta, Legian, Seminyak, and Nusa Dua. Bali experiences two seasons – a wet season from roughly October through April and a dry season from April to October. Even during the rainy season, Bali is still incredibly hot with temperatures in the 90s (30s Celsius) quite common, though the central part of the island often has cooler, damper weather.

Infrastructure in Bali (and in Indonesia as a whole) is slowly improving. The last few years have seen construction of larger highways and bridges connecting different parts of the island of Bali. However, congestion from traffic remains a major problem. There is no subway or rail network on the island of Bali. A public bus system is in place, but has not been as popular or successful as those in larger cities like Jakarta. Taxis and *beemos* (independent drivers) remain common options for those lacking their own transport.

Why Bali?

Bali is world-famous as a prime vacation destination. However, more and more people are choosing to make it their home. Many come on vacation and never want to leave. Large numbers of Australians take advantage of the relatively low cost of living and the proximity to their home country (Bali is just a three- and half-hour flight from Perth or six-hour flight from Sydney). While much further removed from North America, Bali is also becoming increasingly popular with American and Canadian expats who choose to retire abroad or work as digital nomads. There are a variety of visa options that make staying in the country long-term very feasible. The beaches, temples, and waterfalls, and exotic Hindu culture all help it to look every bit the part of the island paradise that it is. The food is nothing short of incredible with cheap local options alongside some world-class restaurants. Whether you want a luxury villa or a small studio, Bali offers a full range of accommodation options to fit any budget. Best of all, the people are warm, friendly, and always laughing.

Why this book?

This book is designed to provide information to help you lay the groundwork for getting into Bali, such as securing visas and finding accommodation. It includes important details you'll need for your first six months in the country, such as getting your driver license, securing a vehicle, and shopping for home goods. It also includes suggestions on different parts of the island that you can choose to settle. Popular locations, such as Seminyak, Canggu, and Nusa Dua are all top choices. However, they are becoming increasingly busy and expensive. This books aims to highlight some out of the way locales and some lesser-known housing options that can save you some money. One of the great things about living in Bali is the relatively low cost of living. Moving all the way to this island paradise just to pay New York or San Francisco prices doesn't make any sense.

As wonderful as Bali is, like anywhere, it is not without its challenges. While this book aims to highlight all the fantastic things you can experience here and ease your transition to life in your new home, it also seeks to paint a realistic picture of some of the difficulties associated with moving abroad- particularly those you will experience here in Bali. Like any new place, there's always going to be an adjustment period. Having said that, it's best to go in with your eyes wide open and prepared for the challenges that you may encounter.

The time I've spent in Bali has been nothing short of amazing! If you choose to make this island your home, I hope you'll love it just as much. Let's get started on this new journey...

CHAPTER 1: GETTING LEGAL – VISAS

Southeast Asia is beautiful, cheap, and there are few things that you can't get if you're willing to part with the money to do so. In this chapter, I'll go over the different options for entering and staying in Bali – the white, the black, and the grey. The visa system in Indonesia is somewhat complicated and corruption is still very much a part of all aspects of life here. This chapter will provide an overview of different types of visas available to those wishing to migrate to Indonesia. The focus will be on the easiest way to make living on the beautiful island of Bali as easy as possible. While this chapter endeavors to touch on all the options available, certain visas (like the marriage or student visas) will not be covered in detail. As the rules are somewhat murky and can be very malleable, it is always best to consult an immigration attorney or certified visa agent to assist you with the process. This chapter aims to give you the information necessary to be as well-informed as possible when you seek out further assistance.

Those entering Bali for holiday are usually issued a visa on arrival. If you are simply spending a week or ten days in Bali, then the visa on arrival tourists is what you will be issued. It is free, valid for 30 days, and CANNOT be extended. There are fines for overstaying your visa, so make sure that you only get this visa if you are certain your trip will be less than 30 days. Since you're looking to spend an extended time in Bali, this is not the visa you want. Listed below are some other options. Remember that you will need to have a minimum of six months validity in your passport when arriving in Indonesia.

Visa on Arrival (Extendable)

This visa costs $35 and is valid for 30 days (including the day on which you arrive in Bali). It can be renewed once for an additional 30 days – allowing you to stay in Bali for a total of 60 days. The fee for the visa extension is $35. There are visa agents all over Bali that will renew your visa for a fee. Some charge as little as $25 or $30, while others will charge over $100. Please note that the visa agent's fee is in addition to the fee that the government charges for renewal. However, it is incredibly simple to extend the visa yourself. You will need to go to the immigration office in Bali closest to the address that you have listed on your arrival card. There are offices in Kuta, Renon, Nusa Dua, and Singaraja (in the north of Bali). I have used the offices in Kuta and Renon and always found the process fairly easy to navigate.

Things happen slowly in Bali, so give yourself ample time for the renewal process. Going to the immigration office ten days before your first 30-day visa expires is a good idea. Remember to be respectful of the local culture when you arrive in the office. Many sun-drenched tourists show up in board shorts, a tank-top or bikini top, and a pair of sandals. They are often refused entry into the office. If you are entering a government building, dress appropriately. You don't have to wear a suit, but I always wear a pair of light cotton pants, a polo shirt, and a pair of shoes. Bear in mind, that your initial visit to the office will just be for your application. You will need to return twice more (usually spaced three days apart) to complete the process. You will likely have a short interview where they will ask you why you want to stay in Bali and if you are working. Any generic answer to the first question should do just fine. *"Indonesia is so beautiful, and I want to visit other islands outside of Bali. So, I need more time."* The answer to the second question is always, *"No, I'm not working."* This is very important as working on this type of visa is strictly prohibited.

Now, your visa on arrival is valid for 60 days in total. In order to stay longer in Bali, you will need to do a visa run. Visa runs are cheap, easy, and incredibly common. For years, many people have stayed in Bali permanently (or semi-permanently) simply by extending their visa on arrival in perpetuity. As of the time of writing, this is completely legal. It is important to note that the visa laws in Indonesia change frequently. With the visa on arrival program suspended as a result of Covid-19, the government may initiate changes when they bring it back. In the past, the government has shown a willingness to crack down on those working illegally in Bali, so this is always a possibility. As of now, it's still an option to stay long-term if you are willing to do a visa run every 60 days.

The Visa Run

After 60 days, you've gotta go. But the good thing is, you can come right back! Unlike in Europe, where the Schengen clock begins ticking after your 90 days, there's no limit to how much time you can spend in Bali. You can continue to renew your visa by jumping on a cheap and short flight to another country. The most popular options are Singapore and Malaysia because of their proximity and low cost. Some people choose to go to Thailand, Vietnam, or the Philippines. Many Australians don't mind making the relatively quick flight home every 60 days to check in on family and friends.

If you choose to pass your time in Bali by extending your visa on arrival every 60 days, you avoid the hassle and cost of the application for other types of visas. You can come and go as you please. Each time you arrive back in Indonesia, you simply pay another $35 for the visa on arrival, and you reset the clock for another 30 days. If you're new to Bali, it gives you the opportunity to get out of the country every two months. I know some people who have been in Bali for a very long time but actually look forward to the opportunity to get out every 60 days.

Travel Options

NOTE: YOU MUST LEAVE INDONESIA – NOT JUST THE ISLAND OF BALI. Flying to Java or another island in Indonesia is not considered a visa run.

There are several low-cost carriers that offer flights to neighboring countries. I usually fly with *Air Asia*. However, there are other airlines that also offer cheap flights, such *Lion Air*, *Garuda*, and *Sriwijaya*.

My preference for Air Asia is that Kuala Lumpur is their hub. You can fly direct from Bali to KL. These flights usually arrive in the low-cost carrier terminal (LCCT) at Kuala Lumpur Airport. While you simply need to get your passport stamped, I often enjoy going into the city for the day. Kuala Lumpur International Airport is about 45 kilometers (less than 30 miles) from the capital city. Kuala Lumpur City Center (KLCC), Bukit Bintang, and Chinatown are all fantastic places to spend the day or get a hotel for the night.

Another popular option for its proximity to Bali is Singapore. Flights from Bali to Singapore take two hours. Changi airport is consistently voted among the best airports in the world. So, it's not a bad place to pass a few hours while you wait for your return flight back to Bali. If you do want to spend the night, you won't regret it. Singapore is a city that everyone should experience at least once. It offers amazing shopping, restaurants, and it's so clean that it's almost sterile. Remember, no spitting or gum chewing allowed in Singapore!

Taking the MRT to the city center is the most cost-effective option. Taxis are metered and the cost to the city center should run you less than $20 USD. Bear in mind that Singapore is not a cheap city! If you are after a little luxury, there are beautiful hotels on Orchard Road. You'll be in the heart of the city and have everything at your doorstep. Check consolidators (like Trivago or Agoda) for reduced rates. If you are on a budget, the section of

Singapore known as *Little India* offers cheaper options, amazing culture, and some of the best food in Singapore.

There are other nearby options for your visa runs – including Hong Kong, Thailand, Vietnam, Cambodia, or Taiwan. All of these locations require a bit more travel time (making them less ideal for a visa run). Flight times of four to five hours each way would make a long day of traveling. If you want to explore a bit of this region, it would be a good idea to spend a few days in the aforementioned locations before returning to Bali. This will give you the time to truly enjoy everything they have to offer. Again, if you just want to get back to Bali ASAP, then Kuala Lumpur or Singapore are the best options.

Social Visa (B211 Visa)

The social visa is a favorite option for many expats living in Indonesia. In the past, it has been available to foreigners entering Indonesia for a variety of purposes – such as conducting business talks, investigating opportunities for investment in Indonesia, exploring Indonesian arts and culture, visiting family, or simply touring the country. The Covid-19 pandemic has changed these restrictions. This visa is now only issued for foreigners who are exploring some type of business opportunity in the country. Due to these changes, it is often referred to as a business visa. That doesn't necessarily mean you need to be engaging in business. You can be granted the visa for the purposes of looking at property that you may be interested in or exploring potential opportunities within Indonesia. If you work with a visa agent, they will handle all of this for you.

This visa is valid for 60 days. However, it can be renewed four times (for an additional 30 days each time). That brings the total validity of the social visa to six months. It's important to note that this is a single-entry visa. That means that you are not permitted to leave Indonesia and come back. Once you pass through immigration to leave the country, you will need to apply for a new visa. In the past, people who had this type of visa were forced to leave the country after all their extensions were exhausted (six months) and reapply offshore for another social visa. This was all done in a manner similar to the visa run for the visa arrival. However, the Indonesian government has recently changed these regulations to allow foreigners to apply for a new social visa while in the country. This effectively allows you to stay in Indonesia indefinitely.

Requirements for B-211 Social Visa

- A valid passport with at least six months of validity (some visa agencies suggest 12 months validity)
- One blank page in the passport for your Indonesian visa
- Two passport-sized photos on a white background (Don't smile in your picture!)
- Letter of invitation from an Indonesian citizen or organization
- Copy of KTP (Indonesian Identity Card) for the person signing the letter of invitation
- Copy of travel itinerary (entering and leaving Indonesia)
- Completed Application
- Proof of Funds (at least $1,500 USD)
  - This comes at the recommendation of visa agents. I have never been asked to show proof of funds for a social visa application.

Drawbacks of the Social Visa

The biggest downside of the social visa is that you're a sort of 'permanent guest' in Indonesia.

- You don't have any discounted access to Indonesian medical care.
- You can't purchase a car or a motorbike in your name.

- You are ineligible for an Indonesian driver license.
- You can't open a bank account.
- Your visa is a single-entry visa (meaning you can't come and go as you please without having to apply for a new visa).
- Repeated cost and paperwork.
  - The application fee for a social visa is approximately $70 USD. This grants you a 60-day visa. However, this assumes that you're able to procure the necessary documents (including the letter of invitation) on your own. Without contacts in Indonesia, this becomes incredibly difficult (if not impossible). Utilizing a visa agent saves time and headaches. However, these agents come with a fee attached. Expect to pay anywhere from $250 to $400 USD for your initial 60-day application.
  - As previously mentioned, you can extend this visa four times for 30 days each time (or a total of six months). You are required to pay the extension fee of approximately $30 USD for each extension. This requires a trip to immigration each month. Alternatively, you can employ an agent to handle all of this for you. The service fees these agents charge will vary, but expect somewhere in the neighborhood of $55 to $75 USD per extension (including the immigration office fee). You need to submit your application for the extension a week to two weeks in advance of the visa's expiration (giving yourself more time in Indonesia is always advisable). Even if you use an agent, you will still

be required to attend one meeting at your local immigration office where you will be fingerprinted and submit to a short interview. This takes place when you do your first visa extension. At present, tourism is not a valid reason for this visa to be granted. Therefore, you should **NOT** mention tourism or work when speaking to immigration. You must be in Indonesia for the purpose of evaluating potential business or investment opportunities.

Addressing Drawbacks of the Social Visa

You don't have any discounted access to Indonesian medical care.

I wouldn't wish Indonesian medical care on my worst enemy. You're really not missing anything here. The KITAS visas (more below) offer discounted medical care. However, these are not very substantial discounts and private insurance is still advisable regardless of your visa.

You can't purchase a car or a motorbike in your name.

This can be an inconvenience – particularly if you plan to make Indonesia your home. If you're not living in a place where you can walk everywhere you need to go, you will need some form of transportation. Motorbikes are the most common type of transport in Bali. Without the opportunity to purchase your own, you will be left with two options: renting or using someone else's identity card to buy something in their name. Renting motorbikes in Bali is incredibly common. You will find plenty of people who will offer rentals (albeit at inflated prices). I will recommend some options for rentals in chapter five. However, a motorbike rental should cost you no more than 500,000 IDR to 1,000,000 IDR per month. This makes your monthly transportation cost incredibly manageable – even without purchasing. If you buy something in someone else's name, remember that they own the bike or car – not you. Make sure you trust them and are willing to lose whatever you've invested in the vehicle.

You are ineligible for an Indonesian driver license.

You can bring international driving licenses to Bali, and they are accepted by the police here. If you get your license at the American Automobile Club (AAA), they should cost about $20 and are valid for one year. You can purchase several to cover future years.

You can't open a bank account.

Without a permanent visa, you won't be able to open an Indonesian bank account. This means that you will have to make withdrawals at local ATMS that accept foreign bank cards.

Multiple Entry Business Visa (B212)

The multiple entry business visa is similar to the aforementioned social visa (B211). The length of stay permitted, and the requirements are slightly different. The multiple entry business visa is valid for one year. However, the holder of the visa cannot remain in Indonesia for longer than 60-days at any one time. This means you need to get out of the country (essentially do a visa run) every 60 days. Some friends of mine have had this visa and they love it. They don't deal with immigration every month. They simply hop on a plane every two months and go to Singapore or KL for the night.

Despite its name, you are NOT permitted to work on this business visa. In this regard, it's the same as the social visa. Your passport will need to be valid for a longer period of time (20 months). Further, you will need to have an average balance of $10,000 USD in your bank account.

KITAS – Temporary Stay Visas

There are several different types of KITAS. The requirements for each is somewhat different.

Marriage

Those who take an Indonesian spouse can apply for a KITAS and also have a fast-track to a permanent residence card. As this book is aimed at those pursuing retirement or early retirement in Indonesia, we are not exploring this visa in detail. However, it is an option for those who are married to an Indonesian.

Retirement Visa

The Indonesian retirement visa is open to anyone over age 55 with sufficient income from a pension or social security. This visa will not allow you to work in Bali. It is a KITAS – or temporary stay visa. It is valid for one year and can be extended for up to five years in total. Each renewal requires a trip to immigration to submit the renewal application. This visa offers a lot of advantages over the social visa or people simply doing visa runs.

<u>Banking</u>: With a KITAS, you can open a bank account in your name at an Indonesian bank. This offers tremendous convenience when compared with making purchases on a credit card or utilizing an ATM to access your international accounts. Many parts of Bali still function as a cash society, so credit cards are not always ideal. Making withdrawals from international accounts is certainly possible. However, not all ATMs in Bali accept international bank cards. Those that do often have a fee attached to them (in addition to any fee that your bank may charge you for an international withdrawal). Considering that most ATMs are capped at 3 million rupiah per withdrawal (about $215 at the time of writing), these fees can really add up. Having easy access to your cash in a local bank is a great way to avoid this.

<u>Driver Licenses:</u> If you've traveled to Bali before, then you're familiar with police roadblocks. If you haven't, then you're in for treat. It is very common for police to set up roadblocks where they check drivers to ensure that their car or motorbike is properly

registered, and they have the correct driver license. These are essentially shakedowns for bribes. Those bribes are usually small, but the whole process of negotiating how much you're going to pay is a headache that you don't want to deal with. Having a KITAS allows you to get an Indonesian license that will help you avoid this.

Healthcare: I'll go into more detail about healthcare in chapter three. It is important to note that those on a tourist visa will a higher price for access to healthcare. Those who hold a KITAS receive a discounted rate for services.

Requirements for the Retirement Visa

- Age 55 or Older
- Completed Application Form (2 Copies)
    - Can Be Found on the Indonesian Embassy Website
- Passport Photos (2) on White Background
    - Do Not Smile or Show Your teeth in the Photo (Really!)
- Proof of Life Insurance
- Proof of Third-Party Liability Insurance
- Proof of Health Insurance
- Rental Agreement (minimum of one year)
- Bank Statements or Proof of Pension
    - Totaling $18,000 USD per annum (or $1,500 per month)
- Letter from an Authorized Indonesia Travel Agent
- Limited Stay Authorization Letter from the Indonesian Directorate General
- Contract to Hire (at least) One Domestic Worker
    - For Example: A Maid or a Driver

What happens after five years?

After five years, you are eligible to apply for permanent residency card (also known as a KITAP). This does NOT require yearly extensions. You simply renew it every five years.

Investor Visa

Those willing to make a significant investment in Indonesia can apply for an investment visa. At the time of writing the minimum investment required is approximately 1 billion rupiah (about $70,000 USD). The Indonesian government restricts the types of work that you can do on an investor visa. For example, if your plan is to open a mom-and-pop café and you are going to the only one running it, this won't qualify under the investor visa. As the name implies, you are simply an investor. In the last twenty years, I've spent a tremendous amount of time in Indonesia. I've seen friends who run businesses become incredibly wealthy. I've also seen friends lose everything to corrupt business practices and antiquated methods of governing. I have chosen to avoid making significant investments in Indonesia.

Student Visa

Those who choose to study in Indonesia can apply for a student visa. There are several universities on the island of Bali. *Universitas Udayana* is the largest university. While the Indonesian education system does not rank well globally in most fields, there are many great opportunities for academics to pursue research on the island. I know several graduate students who've completed the research component of their degree in Bali (including a PhD student from Japan earning a degree in anthropology, a PhD student from America earning her degree in rural education, and MA student from Canada earning his degree in music who studied the Balinese *gamelan*). A student KITAS would entitle the holder to all the same benefits (banking, driver license, and healthcare). Similarly, it does not allow for employment.

Which visa is for me?

This is largely a matter of preference. Overall, I am a big fan of the social visa for its flexibility, cost, and ease of acquisition. It's for these reasons that it is so popular among foreigners. While you don't have many of the conveniences that the KITAS offers (banking, drivers licenses, owning a car / motorbike, or discounts on healthcare), these things are far from a necessity in Bali. What's more, if you are able to secure a KITAS (for example through work), you can access some of these services (such as opening a bank account and maintain it – even after your KITAS expires.

If you were immigrating to an EU country, having legal residence would grant you access to outstanding public healthcare. Indonesia is still a developing nation, so this is not the case. The costs of acquiring and extending the visa are a downfall of the social visa. However, the longer you stay in Indonesia, the more likely you are to acquire local contacts and not need the services of a visa agent. If you are over 55 and opt for the retirement visa, remember that you still need to employ at least one Indonesian domestic worker, and there is a cost attached to that. If you want to employ a driver, gardener, or domestic worker, then this may be the better option for you.

When you are getting started, I believe it helps to have a visa agent. There are MANY visa agents in Bali willing to help foreigners acquire visas. Some are better than others. While I am not affiliated with, nor do I recommend any particular agent, you may try:

Bali Business Consulting

CekIndo Business International

Visa Agent Bali

CHAPTER 2: SHOW ME THE MONEY – BANKING & TAXES

Banking

If you hold a KITAS, you are able to open an Indonesian bank account. This has a lot of advantages because Indonesian ATMs generally limit withdrawals to anywhere between 1,500,000 to 3,000,000 IDR. This requires several trips per month to the ATM (depending on your lifestyle and living expenses). If you're using a foreign bank card, you will have a transaction fee attached to each withdrawal. Transaction fees from Indonesian banks are often negligible, but if your bank charges a foreign transaction fee, this can really add up.

Banking Options

If you are a KITAS holder, you'll have a wealth of banking options in Bali. Popular options include Bank Central Asia (BCA), Bank Mandiri, Bank Negara Indonesia (BNI), and Bank CIMB. I chose BCA as it has a wealth of ATMs throughout Bali and Jakarta. The fees are low, and the service has been quite good.

Setting Up an Account

To set up your account, you will need to go to the main branch of the bank where you are opening your account. For BCA, this is on Jalan Raya Kuta No. 55X. While there are other BCA branches throughout Bali, you must go to this main branch to open your account. You'll need to bring your passport and your KITAS. If you're on an employment KITAS, you may be required to provide additional documentation (such as your employment contract or proof of your residence). I only needed to provide my passport and KITAS. I also needed to complete the account application.

It is important to note that Indonesian banks (and many other businesses in Indonesia) verify identity by matching signatures on identity documents. You must sign your name on your account application *exactly* as you signed it on your passport. When I opened my account, I signed my passport with my middle initial. I subsequently renewed my passport while in Indonesia and did not sign my new passport with the middle initial. It wasn't an issue until I went into the bank to do some banking. I was told that the signatures did not match, so I needed to close my account and open an entirely new account. Fortunately, I managed to squeeze a middle initial onto my passport signature and the lady at the bank looked the other way. However, this is something to keep in mind while in Indonesia. Always ensure that you sign all documents in the same exact way.

ATMs for Foreign Cards

If you are opting to stay in Indonesia on a social visa, business visa, or visa on arrival, you will not be able to open an Indonesian bank account. While you can use credit cards in some locations, Indonesia is still very much a cash society. Even those merchants that do accept credit cards often add a transaction fee to your purchase. Many small local stores and eateries will only accept cash. Therefore, you will need to withdraw cash from ATM machines in Bali. As previously mentioned, these machines often have fairly low withdrawal limits (around 3,000,000 IDR per withdrawal). That means that you will need to pay the foreign transaction fee every time you make a withdrawal. At the time of writing, 3,000,000 IDR is equivalent to around $210 USD. It is important to note that not all ATMs accept foreign cards. In addition to finding an ATM that accepts foreign cards, it is best to find a bank machine that allows for the largest withdrawals. This will help you make fewer withdrawals and minimize your transaction fees. Not all BCA machines accept foreign cards, but the machine at the main branch in Kuta does and has a 2,500,000 IDR limit. Many of the CIMB banks have the most generous withdrawal limits that I've seen. I use the ATM at the CIMB branch on Jalan Bypass Ngurah Rai in Sanur. It has a limit of 3,000,000 IDR.

You can also keep an eye out for ATMs from Western banks – such as Commonwealth and Citibank. These banks often take foreign bank cards. Further, they're the only bank machines that I've ever had any luck cash advancing a credit with. Unfortunately, the only Citi location in Bali is in the heart of Denpasar on Jalan Teuku Umar. On the other hand, Commonwealth has several ATMs throughout the south of Bali from Kuta going up the west coast toward Kerobokan, out in Nusa Dua, and in Sanur.

Cash Advancing Credit Cards

In the event that you run into an emergency situation, you can cash advance your credit card at many banks in Bali. There is a fee attached to it. However, you can access larger amounts of cash. I have used Bank BNI on Jalan Danau Toba in Sanur. I was able to get a cash advance for 8,000,000 IDR. Not all Indonesian banks will do this and the ones that do charge you a fee (usually around 3%). This is in addition to what your credit card company charges you. I strongly advise only using this option in emergency situations. While you may be able to cash advance your credit card at home at ATM machines, I've found this to be problematic in Bali as many ATMs do not accept my American Express or Mastercard.

Beware of Fraud

There is a tremendous amount of fraud at ATM machines in Indonesia. Many thieves will attach devices to the machine to get your card's details. It's always a good idea to use an ATM inside of a bank whenever possible. These machines often have a *satpam* (or security guard) monitoring them. The employees at my bank in Bali once told me that a good safeguard against fraud was to remove my card after my transactions were complete. Then, reinsert the card and enter an incorrect PIN. Then, cancel the transaction and remove my card. The rationale behind this was that if any device was linked to the machine, it would only match the most recent PIN with my card information. I can't say how much truth there is to this, but it was a simple step that made me feel better. Fortunately, I never had any of my card information stolen.

Tax Rates & Residency

For those individuals who are tax residents of Indonesia, the country employs a progressive tax system. The following rates apply to different levels of taxable income:

INCOME	TAX RATE
Up to 50,000,000 IDR	5%
50,000,000 – 250,000,000 IDR	15%
250,000,000 – 500,000,000 IDR	25%
Above 500,000,000 IDR	30%

According to Price Waterhouse Coopers, Indonesia is now offering tax incentives to foreigners who meet certain skill requirements. These individuals may be eligible to only be taxed on their Indonesian sourced income. Foreign sourced income would be taxed in the individual's home country. Different rates and benefits apply to those who are wishing to create an Indonesian company. How you wish to pursue your visa and tax residency is a personal decision that you will have to make. Many people living in Bali choose not to take advantage of Indonesian social services and simply stay on a social visa or a business visa. These individuals report no income and pay no taxes. There is of course a risk to this. Any income producing activities must be kept secret, and there is always the chance you could be caught and deported. In reality, it is so widespread in Bali – particularly among digital nomads. If you were caught, it would more than likely result in your having to pay a bribe to the appropriate official. Just bear in mind that there is a risk involved if you choose to work remotely and live in Bali.

CHAPTER 3: JUST WHAT THE DOCTOR ORDERED – HEALTHCARE AND HEALTH INSURANCE

The healthcare in Bali has improved by leaps and bounds since I first came here over twenty years ago. Having said that, it leaves a LOT to be desired. This needs to be a serious consideration for anyone who is seeking to live in Bali full-time. Many doctors lack proper training. In the past, government initiatives have actually prevented foreign doctors from coming to Indonesia to practice medicine. Basic medical services are available and, as I said, are improving. However, horror stories abound from expats who've received medical treatment in Indonesia (I have a few myself). As far as pharmaceuticals are concerned, many medications are available in Indonesia in both their generic and brand forms. However, there are a great deal of counterfeit medications in Indonesia. So, it is important to go to a reputable pharmacy or hospital to have your prescription filled.

Starting Out (Travel Insurance)

If you are heading to Bali simply to do an exploratory mission, you will likely use travel insurance. Whatever company you choose, ensure that it includes a provision for emergency evacuation. Many services are not available in Indonesia. In the past, I've used *World Nomads*, and I was quite satisfied. They offer decent coverage limits, riders for those participating in dangerous sports, and they made it really easy for me to extend my coverage when I decided to stay in Bali a bit longer. They offer basic and explorer plans. The big difference in these plans seems to be related to trip cancellation, delay, luggage, etc. As far as medical coverage is concerned, the big difference is the levels of evacuation insurance. The explorer plan covers up to half a million USD, while the basic covers only $300,000 USD. For a 40-year-old male, the difference in premiums is roughly $100 USD per month. The basic goes for around $100 USD per month and the explorer for $200 USD. Check their website for up-to-date rates and coverage limits.

When I travel to Europe, I use *Squaremouth*. They are far cheaper and, as a result, offer a lot less coverage. If you're going to a European country with a strong public health system, lower coverage limits may be adequate. However, this is not advisable for Indonesia. Again, whatever travel insurance you choose, ensure that it includes evacuation coverage.

Global Expat Insurance

With the rapid increase in remote workers and international retirees, many insurance companies have responded by creating products for expatriates. Many companies such as *BUPA, Cigna Global*, and *Geo Blue* (from *Blue Cross and Blue Shield*) offer this type of coverage. Americans are always at a disadvantage as far as healthcare is concerned. Healthcare, and as a result health insurance, is more expensive than anywhere else in the world. For Americans, a big advantage of these types of insurance products is that they cover you for a limited amount of time in the USA. I have a friend who has the Cigna Global Silver Plan. She pays $200 per month and is covered for up to 180 days in the USA. Her plan includes $1 million in coverage, wellness checks, and evacuation and repatriation. The BUPA plans that I've looked at offer the option to exclude coverage in the USA. If you choose to include America in your coverage, the premium is MUCH higher. A healthy 40-year-old can generally get excellent coverage from BUPA (excluding America) for around $200 per month. Another option that expats can explore is *MedJet*. I've found their rates to be reasonable. However, for those wishing to make Bali a long-term home, their products may not be ideal. For example, the five-year policy / membership restricts the insured to spending only 90 consecutive days abroad. There is a one-year policy that allows the insured to be abroad for the entire year. Check their website for details and see if it is appropriate for your situation.

KITAS Discount

While I prefer the cost, convenience, and flexibility of the social visa, there are some advantages to the KITAS. As far as medical coverage is concerned, there are many doctors and hospitals that offer preferential rates for holders of a KITAS. When you go to a provider to seek medical care, one of the questions they ask when they take your personal information is if you have a KITAS. Of course, they are supposed to check your KITAS – some do, but some don't.

The nice thing about being registered with a medical provider as being eligible for the KITAS discount is that they usually only check your KITAS when you sign up. I've showed my KITAS when signing up at a hospital and was able to receive the KITAS discount years later (when I was actually on a social visa). To be clear, with or without the KITAS discount, most basic medical procedures won't break the bank in Bali.

Self-Insured Expats

I have a very good friend in Bali who chooses to self-insure. While there is tremendous risk associated with this, it may be a good value for some – particularly those who are young and healthy. My friend carries coverage only for catastrophic events, and his policy includes evacuation insurance. He simply covers normal medical expenses out of his own pocket. He is also a citizen of an EU country with an excellent public health system. His feeling is that if he were to get a serious illness or disease (something like cancer), he would simply fly back to Europe where he would receive free treatment. While Americans living abroad can come back to the states and should be able to enroll in Affordable Care Act (ACA) coverage at any time (as a move back to America is usually considered a qualifying life event), this is a complicated and expensive scenario. Again, this is a decision that you will need to make based on your own healthcare needs and financial resources.

Care Providers in Bali

Where you choose to receive medical care in Bali will probably be based on several factors – where you're located, the severity of your condition, and your ability to pay. There are many facilities that advertise Western standards of care. In many ways, they are more Western. However, they are certainly not equivalent to the standard of care received at home.

BIMC

BIMC in Kuta was the first hospital in Bali to offer 'Western' standards of medical care. They now have two other locations in Nusa Dua and in Ubud. I have been treated there several times. I even spent a night in the hospital there with dengue fever. In some cases, they were able to provide adequate levels of care. Having said that, they are quite expensive by Bali standards. I paid $800 USD for the night I spent there. BIMC does offer a privilege membership card that costs about $50 USD per year and offers substantial discounts. If you do choose to use their services, this does seem like a good value. They also offer a loyalty card which is entirely free and offers some discounts. However, these discounts are not as substantial as the paid membership.

Siloam

Siloam is relatively new when compared with BIMC. They also offer one of the widest arrays of testing and services in Bali. As a result, they are very popular with expats. The cost of their services are not cheap. Like BIMC, they offer

Sanglah Hospital

Sanglah is the public hospital where many locals receive medical care. They are located in Denpasar. I have never received care there. However, many of my Balinese friends have been treated there and been quite satisfied. I visited a friend there and was not entirely impressed.

Kasih Ibu

Graha Asih

Apotek/Pharmacy

For many smaller problems, you can often get assistance at a local pharmacy (*apotek*). While you'll find many small pharmacies throughout Bali, *Kimia Farma* is the largest chain (located all throughout Indonesia). In many cases, the pharmacist will be able to offer some assistance and suggest a medication to help you. Prescriptions are usually not required (even when the medication says 'only by prescription'). This is often the most cost-effective method for dealing with small problems. Pharmacists will usually give you the brand-name medication first. It's always good practice to ask if the generic is available (at a fraction of the cost).

Another great thing about the *Kimia Farma* locations is that many have doctors inside. I once had something lodged on my cornea. I went to a *Kimia Farma* in *Tuban* that had an ophthalmologist's office inside. She was able to remove the debris from my eye and give me antibiotics – all for around $20 (no insurance). Different pharmacies have different doctors' offices inside. I saw a physical therapist at a *Kimia Farma* in Denpasar and received excellent treatment. The pharmacist can often refer you to the location that has the specialist you require.

Common Health Concerns

Like anywhere else in the world, there are some things to be aware of Bali to always ensure that you're in the best possible health. Fortunately, most concerns are minor ones.

Motorbike accidents

Most foreigners in Bali visit a healthcare provider for motorbike accidents. While these can be serious, most are minor cuts and scrapes. Wear a helmet and be sure to clean out any wounds. Always keep your cuts bandaged – especially on your feet if you wear sandals.

Bali Belly

Many Westerners have a reaction to the food in Bali. The local cuisine may contain bacteria that your body may not be used, resulting in several unexpected trips to the toilet. For those new to Bali, you may choose to avoid street food. Never drink the tap water in Bali – bottled water only!

Malaria

Malaria is not currently a serious concern in Bali. If you travel to more remote areas of Bali or to the outer islands, you may need to take precautions. Some areas of Indonesia suffer from terrible rates of Malaria infection. Talk to your doctor to see what precautions or medications you need to take. Wearing good mosquito repellant and long pants and sleeves (particularly at dusk) is also important.

Dengue Fever

Unfortunately, Dengue fever is a problem in Bali. Having had it before, I can tell you that it is an absolutely awful illness. There is a vaccine available, however it may not be available or approved in all countries. Talk to your doctor about what precautions you should take. Again, good mosquito repellant and taking precautions to avoid bites are always a good idea.

Rabies

Rabies is a problem in Bali. If you are bitten by a dog or potential host, you should contact a local doctor to see if you need Rabies treatment.

Sexually Transmitted Infections (STIs)

There is a lot of prostitution in Bali. As a result, there is a risk of sexually transmitted infections.

Vaccines

Before you leave for Bali, it's a good idea to check with your doctor to see what vaccinations are required or suggested for your trip.

CHAPTER 4: SOME LIGHT HOUSEWORK – FINDING ACCOMMODATION IN BALI

When moving to Bali, you're going to need to make the decision to rent or to buy accommodation. I would not suggest organizing long-term accommodation before you arrive in Bali (unless you have someone that you know and trust in Bali working on your behalf). If you book accommodation online, you are likely going to overpay. You also may be disappointed to learn that the accommodation you arrive to does not meet your expectations. Bali is quite simply my favorite place on Earth. I first came here over twenty years ago. I've had multiple opportunities to buy a home here and have turned down every single one with no regrets. Remember that the country is rife with corruption. I would only invest money in Bali that you are fully prepared to lose. Organize an apartment on Airbnb, Booking, or through one of the many Facebook groups for Bali expats. You will likely pay a bit more than what you would if you were on the ground in Bali, but you will have a place organized for when you first arrive. You will also have an address for your visa application. I would not book anything for longer than one month.

What type of places are available?

Bali offers a variety of options for accommodation. What you rent will depend first and foremost on your budget. You will also need to determine what part of the island your most interested in calling home. I will cover the pros and cons of some popular locations in chapter 9. First, let's look at some options for living.

Kos

This is the cheapest option that you will find in Bali. A *kos* is really just a small studio apartment. I've stayed in MANY over my years in Bali. They are cheap, generally require no rental contract, and all over the island.

Most Basic Option (400,000 – 500,000 IDR per month)

These rooms usually have no furnishings and a very simple bathroom. There's no heat, aircon, or hot water. The bathroom is usually a squat toilet in a 'wet room' with a large tank that fills up with cold water. You scoop water out of the tank to shower and to flush the toilet. I've stayed in these places short term. They're incredibly cheap and easy to find. If this is your budget, then getting a cheap mattress and throwing it on the floor can give you a real local experience. I've always enjoyed the community that these places offer. It is also a great way to immerse yourself in Indonesian culture and learn the language. Look for signs that say *Terima Kos*

Furnished (1,00,000 – 3,000,000 IDR per month)

These are usually the places where I tend to stay. They require no rental contract and are still very affordable. There are many options available throughout *Kuta*. However, these usually have a higher price tag attached to them. If you go towards the center of the island, you can find great bargains. *Renon* and *Denpasar* have many places available. In *Denpasar, Jalan Nusa Indah* has a wealth of affordable housing. *Jalan Merdeka* in Renon similarly has affordable places. I've stayed at a nice place on *Jalan Nusa Indah* (number 16) for one million per month with a Western bathroom, hot water, air conditioning, and a maid who cleans the room and common areas. Most of these places have no kitchen.

Serviced Apartments (3,00,000 – 7,000,000 IDR per month)

There are more Western-style apartments available in some parts of Bali. You can generally find great options in Denpasar, Sanur, Kerobokan, and Kuta. These are similar to the furnished *kos* listed above, but they usually have a kitchen. They may also have some community amenities, such as a swimming pool. There are several available for rent on *Jalan Wira*, just off *of Jalan Segara Ayu* in *Sanur*. There are also several available just behind the KFC in Sanur. These may or may not require a rental contract, depending on your landlord. Rent is usually paid monthly. Some places may ask for several months in advance. Everything is negotiable in Bali, so keep this in mind as you decide how much you pay.

Local Homes / Villlas (5,000,000 – 100,000,000 IDR per month)

Finding a home or villa for rent is not going to be difficult. Finding one at a good price may prove to be more of a challenge. Many of these places require the year to be paid in full and it is often not cheap. A friend of mine rents a small villa from a local family. She's had the same place for five years. It's a 3-bedroom villa with a swimming pool, and she pays 50,000,000 IDR per year. If you're looking for something similar, it's always best to talk to as many local people as possible. Check *The Bali Advertiser*, a free local paper that is available at many cafes and restaurants. It's also a good idea to check bulletin boards in cafes. Café Moka has several locations throughout the island where people list homes for rent. Also check *Bali Buda*, which also sometimes advertises local accommodation.

You will likely have to sign a rental agreement for these places.

If you do, and there's a substantial sum of money involved, you should have a local friend, or a local attorney look it over. Some families may not ask for a rental agreement. They may want to avoid declaring any rental income from the home. If this is the case, remember that any cash you hand over is done in good faith. I always approach these agreements with the idea that whatever I pay is money that I'm prepared to lose. To this point, I've never had anyone be dishonest with me, but it is always good to be cautious.

Real Estate Offices / Rental Agents

These people don't work for free. If you decide to arrange your accommodation through one of these agencies, it will likely be easier and more transparent. However, that all comes with a price tag attached to it. These places will likely charge several times over what others charge.

What do I need to rent?

What you'll actually need to rent will vary significantly depending on the type of place you rent and who you rent from. I've always stayed with local families. I have paid cash up front when I've had one-year rentals. I've also paid by the month when I've been living in a kos. I've never actually had to sign a rental agreement in Bali. I've also never had a problem with the people I've rented from. If you're choosing to live in a high-price villa, you will likely be asked to sign a rental agreement. In this case, you will need your passport and (if applicable) a copy of your KITAS.

Indonesia has a very antiquated and corrupt court system. As a result, you may find that your rental agreement is about as good as the paper it is written on.

Purchasing a Home

I have been coming to Bali for over twenty years. I've called it home for several of those years. However, I've never purchased a home here. The reason is largely related to the transparency in the purchase process and how foreigners hold title in Indonesia. In this section, I'm going to go over some options for purchasing and holding title in Indonesia. Foreigners cannot legally own land outright in Indonesia. This is what we commonly refer to as *freehold* or *fee simple*. Indonesians refer to this as *hak milk*.

Hak Milik

It is illegal for foreigners to own land in this manner – however, there is a system in place to circumvent these rules. Foreigners can use an Indonesian nominee and purchase the land in their name. I have a friend who owns a beautiful home in Bali under this arrangement. He's had it for over ten years and never had an issue. Having said that, you are placing a tremendous amount of trust in your nominee – regardless of what the contract says. Indonesia is an incredibly corrupt country. There is often a fee paid to the nominee when the property is either bought or sold. This is to be arranged between you and your nominee and should be in writing.

Hak Pakai

This is right of usage and is a great (legal) way for foreigners to buy land in Indonesia. It is registered with the land office and allows the foreign owner rights to the land for up to 80 years. It can even be sold to Indonesians and upgraded to *hak milik*.

Hak Sewa

Sewa is to rent, and hak sewa is leasehold ownership of land. It is legal for foreigners to hold property in this manner. However, once the lease expires, it reverts back to the person who owns the property *hak milik* (freehold).

NOTE: Buying property in Indonesia is incredibly complex and difficult. There are so many cheap options for those wishing to rent. For me, I found purchasing a home to be not worth the risk. Having said that, in the time I've been there, I've met several people who've become millionaires off of their land investments in Bali. I've also met a lot of people who've been ripped off. Make the best decision for your own situation. However, unless you want an expensive, upscale villa, it might be best just to rent something cheap.

Finding a Home

Often the best way to find accommodation (to either rent or to buy) is via word of mouth. Of course, this requires you to be on the island. If you are looking for something online, you can check the following resources below as a starting point on your search for accommodation.

LJ Hooker is an Australian Company with offices around Bali. You can visit their location on Sunset Road or their website at ljhooker.co.id

Bali Moves is a great online resource for rentals or purchases in the Sanur area. Visit them at www.balimoves.com

Ring Bali Property is another realtor located in Sanur. You can visit them at ringbaliproperty.com

U Property Indonesia is an Indonesia company located in Java with a presence in Bali. You can visit them at upropertyindonesia.com

Elite Havens offers luxury villa rentals and management services in the Seminyak / Kerobokan area. They have listings all around Bali. You can visit them at elitehavens.com

Lux Indo Property is located in Seminyak and deals with luxury properties in Bali. You can visit them at luxindoproperty.com

I Lot Property assists with land development and building a villa in Bali. They also assist with property management. You can visit them at www.ilotpropertybali.com

Bali Coconut Living also offers villas for sale or long-term rental around the Seminyak and Canggu area. Visit them at https://balicoconutliving.com/

Ubud Property offers villas for sale or long-term rental. You can visit them at http://www.ubudrentalservice.com/

NOTE: This list is not exhaustive, but will give you a place to start your search. Remember that the price to rent accommodation can range from $40 a month to tens of thousands per month. If you are looking for the absolute cheapest place, you are not going to find it online. It really pays to get to the island. If you want a cheap, local-style place, look for signs that say "TERIMA KOST." Also, check out locations around Denpasar (where many local people live). Be aware that your place is not going to look like a $10,000 per month villa. It's going to be very basic. I usually choose to find a more upscale kos for $100 to $300 per month. You can get a better rate if you pay a year upfront.

Renting v. Buying in Bali

My opinion on this topic is just that – my opinion. I have been coming to Bali for decades and have never purchased a home or land here. In that time, I've undoubtedly missed out on opportunities to make substantial sums of money. I've also avoided scenarios where I may have been ripped off and lost everything. I've been approached by some people who've suggested that we conspire to pay off judges to seize a foreigner's property, then sell it and split the profit. In case the obvious eluded you here, never trust someone who wants to use your money to bribe a judge and steal others' property. They're generally untrustworthy people.

The truth is that rules regarding investment in Indonesia have changed considerably over the last twenty years. Just as they've changed with a stroke of pen, they can just as easily change back. Sure, it's nice to have *your own place* in Bali. However, there are plenty of easy, affordable options for foreigners. There are also long-term leases available. I would not get involved with a local nominee. I've see this happen with disastrous consequences. I've also seen it work out perfectly. However, I am not comfortable taking that risk. If you want the security of long-term accommodation, then consider a long-term rental agreement or purchasing something leasehold.

CHAPTER 5: DUDE, WHERE'S MY MOTORBIKE? – BUYING A MOTORBIKE AND GETTING A DRIVER LICENSE

Once you land in Bali, you'll notice the prevalence of motorbikes on the island. It is without a doubt the preferred method of travel for local people and many expats, too. I've been coming to Bali for over twenty years and have never driven a car here. There are many reasons for this – not the least of which is traffic. However, riding a motorbike presents safety concerns and can be a real inconvenience during the rainy season.

Purchasing a Motorbike

You cannot legally purchase a motorbike in Bali without a KITAS. So, if you come on a social visa or a visa on arrival, you will not be able to buy your own bike. Without a KITAS, your options would either be to rent long-term or to purchase a bike in someone else's name. I've done both. I truly believe that if you're here for any length of time, buying a bike is a great option. Bikes are affordable to purchase and can save you money versus a rental in the long run. Further, you don't have to worry about the costs associated with damaging a rental bike. This can often create complications as the owner may expect an exorbitant amount of compensation for a simple scratch.

What are my options for purchasing a bike?

If you are a legal resident of Bali with a KITAS, you can purchase a motorbike or a car in your own name. Non-Indonesians are usually expected to pay cash (or use a credit card). The process is fairly straightforward and did not even require that I present a driver license. Shortly after you purchase the bike, you will receive your "blue book." This signifies your ownership of the bike. DO NOT LOSE THIS! If you want to sell the bike, you need this document to prove that you are the rightful owner. Some people choose not to collect their book from the dealership, as they believe it is safer in the dealer's possession. Other people leave the blue books for cars or bikes at a bank. Regardless of where you choose to keep yours, ensure that it is in a secure location.

What if I don't have a KITAS?

If you don't have a KITAS and you want to purchase a bike, things become a bit more complicated – but not impossible. You can purchase a bike in the name of an Indonesian person or another Westerner who has a KITAS. Obviously, you want this to be someone you trust. I have done this before and all that I needed to do was present a copy of the identity card (KITAS) to the dealership. I was then able to purchase the bike. However, bear in mind that the bike will be in the name of the person who is on the identity card (as will the blue book). You will probably want to keep the blue book yourself, as this will give you some leverage should you ever have a disagreement with the person whose name you've used to secure the bike. If you are arriving in Bali with some trusted contacts who can assist you, this may work for you. However, if you are new to Bali and don't know anyone, renting a bike may be the smartest move.

Renting a Motorbike

I've rented and I've purchased bikes before. I currently do not own a bike in Bali, and I choose to rent when I arrive in Bali. I have rented from the same trusted friend for the past twenty years. You will find no shortage of people who want to rent to you in Kuta. The prices are going to be incredibly inflated. You may need to get out of Kuta and speak to someone at your hotel. Don't be surprised if daily rates in Kuta hover around 200,000 to 300,000 IDR per day. This is outrageous. A rental should cost no more than 50,000 IDR per day, and better rates are available monthly. Many local people will be more than happy to rent you a bike for 600,000 to 800,000 IDR per month. [NOTE: At the time of writing, 600,000 IDR is approximately $40 USD.]

Another thing to be aware of is insurance. In Kuta, it is a common scam for people to offer you "insurance" with your rental. They will tell you that if the bike is damaged, you will have to pay an exorbitant fee that exceeds the purchase price of a new bike. I have been told $5,000 USD for a bike that was worth less than $1,000. However, if you purchase the insurance, you are only responsible for a $1,000 deductible. In fact, this is not insurance. It is just a way to get extra money out of unsuspecting tourists.

Recognize that riding a bike (or driving) in Bali is a big risk. It is still very much a cash society. Most people you rent from will not care what kind of protection your American Express offers. The best course of action is to be extremely careful when driving and avoid locations and times when streets are busy and packed with intoxicated tourists on motorbikes (e.g.- anywhere in Kuta). If you do find that you've damaged a bike, the best course of action is usually to get it repaired yourself at one of the many shops on the island. If you've damaged a Honda, go to a Honda dealer (as they will have a repair shop). It will be far cheaper and save you a lot of grief.

Where Can I Buy a Bike? What are the choices?

If you do decide to purchase a bike, there are a lot of options. Honda and Yamaha tend to be the biggest brands on the island and offer the most shops for purchase and service. Local people consider Honda to be the best brand, so you will usually pay a bit more for these bikes (though they tend to have a higher resale value). You can check out the following shops:

Astra Motor in Kuta

Honda Tuban on Jalan Raya Tuban

Honda Taman Agung (closer to Canggu)

Yamaha Denpasar on Jalan Diponegoro

Yamaha Nusa Dua Indah on the Bypass

Yamaha Semangat in Seminyak

You can also choose to purchase a bike second hand. Do remember to get a written record of the transaction and a copy of the blue book (as this will show you are the rightful owner of the bike). Be very careful when purchasing a bike second-hand. It is a good idea to take a local person you trust to assist with the transaction.

A Note on Credit v. Cash

Financing is available for purchases of new bikes in Bali. It is usually for Indonesian residents, and the interest rates are astronomical. Remember that there are no truth-in-lending regulations in Indonesia. You will see interest rates advertised that are incredibly low (and also incredibly inaccurate). Do the math. If it sounds too good to be true, it usually is. New bikes are less than $2,000 USD. At the time of writing, a Yamaha Mio costs less than $1,200 USD. I have found it better to bring cash.

Fuel

One of the really nice things about Indonesia is that fuel is subsidized by the government. However, given the rise in global energy prices, the government has not been able to maintain its generous subsidies. As a result, in late 2022, the price of petrol increased (though it remains about half the price of the global average).

Pertalite is the cheapest fuel required of most motorbikes and it runs 10,000 IDR per liter. This is approximately 0.65 USD per liter or $2.46 per gallon.

More expensive versions of fuel include Pertamax and Pertamax Turbo. Occasionally, gas stations will run out of Pertalite, and you may be forced to purchase Pertamax. Expect to pay around 14,500 IDR per liter for this brand of gasoline.

Tolls

If you've traveled around Bali in the last ten to fifteen years, you've noticed a huge increase in the amount of traffic on the roads. The traffic jams are becoming more and more problematic. The government has responded by opening a toll road that connects Denpasar with Tuban (the airport) and Nusa Dua. It cuts out the main area around Kuta and is a big time-saver. It is also a very picturesque ride. It is very important to note that you cannot pay cash at the toll booths. You need to use a card for the toll road that you load up with credit. These cards can be purchased and reloaded at Indo Maret locations. Indo Maret is a chain of Indonesian convenience stores similar to Circle K or 7-11. You can ask for *kartu untuk jalan tol*. Alternatively, you can purchase a card at Bank Mandiri locations. It costs approximately 5,000 IDR for motorbikes to use the toll road.

Driver Licenses

If you have a KITAS, you can apply for a local driver license. This will save you a lot of hassle at police roadblocks (which are common). The Indonesian license (commonly referred to as a SIM) is available at the police station on Jalan Gunung Sanghyang. For a motorbike, you need a Class C SIM. It is valid for five years and costs approximately 100,000 IDR.

If you do not have a KITAS, then you need to arrive in Indonesia with an international driver license. Keep in mind that in most countries, you can drive a 125cc scooter with a regular driver license. That is, you do not need to have a motorcycle (or "heavy bike" license). This is not the case in Indonesia. The international driver license must be stamped for a two-wheeled vehicle (motorcycle) to be accepted by police at roadblocks. Even if the license says that regular cars and motorbikes 125cc and under are covered, you will lose the argument with the cops. You can get an international license at any American Automobile Club (AAA) location for around $15. They are valid for a year from the date on the front. Many places will be happy to make several for you for future years (provided you pay for each one). There are also many online options for obtaining an international license. Again, bear in mind that these licenses need to show that you are legally able to operate a motorcycle.

In earlier times, fake international licenses were very easy to find in Bali. They still exist, but are not as out in the open. When tourists don't have licenses, the police make money. So, the police have an incentive to shut these operations down. For obvious reasons, I cannot mention the few locations where fake licenses can still be found. It usually costs around 250,000 IDR for a one-year license or 1 million IDR (approximately $80) for a license that has a long-term validity (10+ years).

Police Roadblocks

Police often set up roadblocks where they will perform "document checks." These are simply a shakedown for people who do not have local or international driver licenses. Police are becoming a bit more careful given the prevalence of camera phones, but they are still looking for a bribe. In my opinion, it is just part of living in Bali. While they may initially ask for more, 50,000 IDR is the standard bribe if you do not have the appropriate documentation. Given that official fines often cost at least 250,000 IDR, I think this is a bargain. If you are without a helmet (or someone on the back of your bike is without a helmet), you will also be expected to pay. If you don't want to contribute to the corruption, it's best to ensure that you have the appropriate documentation to drive legally.

My Thoughts

If you are comfortable with riding a bike, you may choose to get a bike and just rent a car for a few months during the rainy season. Another very logical option for those who head to Indonesia on a retirement visa is to simply hire a driver. The requirements of the retirement visa stipulate that you must employ one local person. You may choose to simply hire a driver who can use his car to take you where you need to go. This will eliminate the hassle associated with purchasing a car or bike, getting a license, and navigating the roads in Bali!

CHAPTER 6: RETAIL THERAPY – SHOPPING & SHIPPING

For most Westerners, Bali is a half a world away from home. There's only so much you can pack in an extra suitcase. Fortunately, you can get most of what you need here in Bali. There are a few things that you may want to bring in large quantities, as they are either difficult to find or very expensive. When I moved to Bali, I tried to look at my new life as an adventure. Happiness came from all the beautiful things around me – as opposed to the things that I could buy. Taking more of a minimalist perspective isn't the worst thing in the world. Ultimately, you're going to have to adapt to the way of life in Bali if you want to make it your home. So, it is good to get used to what you can source locally. This chapter will cover your shopping options. I'm going to start with my staunch opposition to shipping.

Shipping from Home

Shipping things to Indonesia is an absolute nightmare. What doesn't get stolen often gets delayed in customs. That favorite piece of furniture that you can't live without will probably be better off in a friend's house or a storage unit. Besides, a great deal of furniture is actually made in Indonesia. Visit some local furniture makers in Kerobokan or Ubud to find what you want for your new home. The price and quality might just surprise you!

Things You May Want to Take

This list is going to be different for everyone. I'm going to share some of the things that I wish I would have taken a lot of, as they're expensive or tough to get here in Bali. These are specific to me and my needs. Perhaps they're on your list too!

Medications – There are pros and cons to prescriptions meds in Bali. On the plus side, many medications that require a prescription can be purchased at any *kimia farma apotik* without a prescription. Generic medications can often be bought for next to nothing. However, Indonesia has always had – and continues to have – a problem with quality control for their pharmaceutical industry. There is a tremendous amount of counterfeit medication, and doctors have told me that dosages are not always exact. I have had good luck with kimia farma or purchasing directly from a hospital. I also try to avoid generic whenever possible. If you take a daily medication, try to bring as much as possible from home.

Running Shoes – Cheap running shoes are easy to come by in Bali. However, high-quality running shoes are expensive. If you are a runner and need good shoes, pack a few extra pairs.

Lip Balm – You can find lip balm at any *apotik* (pharmacy) in Bali. I use *Carmex* quite often. In *Wal-Mart*, a 3-pack costs $2.99. In Bali, it is almost impossible to find. If you can find it at all, it is very expensive! If this is something you use often, bring extra.

Cameras and Lenses – If you enjoy photography, you may want to update your equipment before moving to Bali. You can find camera equipment here, but the prices tend to be significantly higher. You also run the risk of getting products that are not genuine.

Laptops – Again, you run the risk of getting products that are not genuine. Genuine, high-quality products are often not all that affordable. If you are going the digital nomad route and need new equipment, update it before you leave.

Deodorant and Toiletries – If you have a brand of deodorant that you are comfortable with, you may want to pack a few extra sticks. Similarly, with a favorite toothpaste or any other toiletries that you require, you may want to bring a bit extra. At the end of the day, if you are living here, you are going to have to adapt to the local choices. Think about what you can and cannot live without.

Malls

Indonesians LOVE malls and 'malling.' In Jakarta, malls are not only places where people go to find the store they need, but they are also a source of recreation. Malls are a fun place to go walk around, get a coffee or an ice cream, and perhaps see a movie. While a few malls started popping up in Bali over twenty years ago, they have now grown in popularity and number. While most Westerners going to Bali are not looking for a shopping mall, you shouldn't be surprised by how common a sight they are on the island. It is also nice if you need something that you might be unable to find elsewhere. I often go to the mall to get my running shoes. Popular malls include:

Beach Walk in Kuta

Discovery in Kartika Plaza

Mal Bali Galeria

Plaza Renon

Nusa Dua Square

Lippo Plaza on Sunset Road

Lippo Mall in Kartika

Housewares

What you require in Bali will depend on what type of accommodation you select. Even if you live in a kos, you will likely need a few things (a mattress, linens, simple dishes and cups, a kettle, a water dispenser, etc...). There are many stores where you can find the essentials for your home.

Makro (Jln Bypass)

Carrefour (Sunset Road)

Ace Hardware (multiple locations)

Canggu and Co Home Store

Dewata Housewares in Denpasar

Lapis Homeware in Kuta

If you are moving to Bali for a real authentic experience and trying to stretch your dollars, then consider renting a kos and getting the bare essentials. You can find almost everything you need at Carrefour on Sunset Road for reasonable prices. I have stayed for months at a time in a small kos with a mattress and two sets of linens. A small fridge can be purchased to keep essentials for breakfast and snacks. As you are unable to drink the tap water, I would suggest getting a 19-liter bottle of drinking water for your home. Aqua is the most popular brand and the large bottles are referred to as 'gallon' in the local shops (even though they are much bigger than a gallon). They cost about 60,000 IDR. You can buy a small pump dispenser at Carrefour to pump your drinking water. This saves you a ton of money and is far better for the environment.

Is it really cheap to live in Bali?

If you adhere to a local standard of living, you will find that almost everything is incredibly cheap in Bali. If you insist on applying a Western standard of living to your life in Bali, you may be surprised at how expensive it really can be. If you go to local shops, you can find things for much cheaper prices, but be prepared to bargain. Much like accommodation and food, there are so many affordable options, but you need to be able to see them as options. Unfortunately with the influx of 'influencers' arriving in Canggu, all showcasing the dream of living in Bali, many people have lost site of what a beautiful and simple life Bali really offers. If you want to live the artificial life that many people present on Instagram, you can. Just keep in mind that there is a hefty price tag attached to that.

CHAPTER 7: ARE YOU GONNA EAT THAT? – FOOD & DRINK

Indonesian food is by far one of my favorite types of cuisine anywhere on Earth! Bali has always been an international hotspot, but it's become increasingly popular in the last several years. As a result, there's tremendous international influence on the islands gastronomy. As this book is aimed at the budget traveler, we're going to begin by covering some popular local dishes.

Popular Indonesian Dishes

Babi Guling

One of the big differences that you'll notice in Bali relative to the rest of Indonesia is the prevalence of pork. As the most populous Muslim nation in the world, pork is not found in most parts of Indonesia. However, Balinese suckling pig (*babi guling*) is a local favorite.

Nasi

Rice is the staple of the Indonesian diet. People will often ask "*Sudah makan nasi?*" which means "Have you already eaten rice?" You will mostly find *nasi putih*, which is white (sticky) rice. In addition, you can find *nasi kuning* (yellow rice) and *nasi merah* (brown rice). *Nasi merah* literally means red rice, but it is the healthiest rice option available at certain restaurants. My personal favorite is *nasi uduk*. It is a white rice that is made with coconut milk and lemongrass. It is not always easy to find, but it is incredibly delicious!

Nasi Goreng

Perhaps the most famous of Indonesian dishes – *nasi goreng* is Indonesia fried rice. It is served with a fried egg. It usually includes vegetables (*sayur*). However, you can often find it with chicken (*nasi goreng ayam*) or goat meat (*nasi goreng kambing*).

Nasi Campur

Campur means "mixed" in Indonesian. So, *nasi campur* is simply mixed rice. It is one of my favorite dishes on the island. There is a restaurant in Sanur on Jalan Segara Ayu that does perhaps the best *nasi campur* on the island. It is rice mixed with a variety of ingredients (from meat to vegetables). It is a can't miss while in Bali!

Ayam Bakar / Goreng

Ayam is chicken in Indonesian. While *bakar* is grilled, *goreng* is fried. I am a big fan of *ayam bakar*. It is usually cooked with *kecap* (a sweet soy sauce) and served with *nasi putih* (white rice) and *lalapan* (a small side of vegetables).

Ikan Bakar / Goreng

Like chicken, fish dishes are also popular both grilled and fried. Be sure to insist on *ikan laut* (fish from the sea), as river fish is popular in many parts of Indonesia. If you are looking for a fantastic grilled fish dinner, you have to go to Jimbaran. Simply ask your taxi driver for *ikan bakar di Jimbaran*.

Bakso

As someone who has spent a ton of time in Bali, I am ashamed to say it, but... I personally hate *bakso*! However, it is an incredibly popular dish. It is a meatball soup (that I don't think is in any way healthy for you), and is often sold by street carts. You will often see people walking around with a *bakso kart*, tapping a spoon on a glass bottle. It is incredibly cheap and remains a local favorite.

Satay (*ayam* or *kambing*) with peanut sauce

Satay ayam is one of my favorite Indonesian dishes. It is grilled chicken skewers served with peanut sauce. It comes with a side of white rice and vegetables (*nasi putih* and *lalapan*). You can also find *satay kambing* (goat) or even *satay ikan* (fish).

Sambal

Sambal is Indonesian chili sauce. It is very spicy and very delicious. When you ask for *sambal* in a restaurant, you are likely to be met with one of two options. The first is a homemade salsa-type chili sauce that is absolutely delicious. The second is a creamy chili sauce from a bottle. While not intolerable, the latter option is not nearly the same as authentic sambal.

Vegetarian Options (Tempeh and Tahu) Earth and Zula, Soul on the Beach (Sanur)

Fast-Food

If you are one of those people who simply can't live without your Western fast-food options, don't worry – Bali has all the popular chains on offer. While I am not a fast-food lover myself, you can find McDonald's, Burger King, KFC, Pizza Hut, and Dunkin all throughout the island.

Coffee

There are literally TONS of cafes popping up everywhere. For those who need their triple soy no foam latte with one pump of vanilla, don't worry – there are plenty of Starbucks locations throughout the island. Personally, I love finding good local cafes, and there are no shortage of these in Bali. One of my absolute favorites is Simply

Brew in Sanur. Other options include The Koop in Seminyak, Kawisari in Canggu, and Black Eye Coffee in Ubud.

Fine Dining

Bali has really stepped up its game since becoming a major international destination for people from all walks of life. It's no longer just a place for traveling surfers and hippie backpackers. There are a lot of fine dining restaurants in Bali, particularly in the Seminyak area. With that said, there are hefty price tags attached to these dining experiences. As this book really focuses on affordable, local options, I won't go into detail here. Just know that these dining experiences are available. You can check out options inside the St. Regis Resort and the Ritz-Carlton.

Wine, Spirits, & Beer

Wine is not cheap and neither are spirits. Beer is relatively cheap. The local beer Bintang is not half bad when it's served iced-cold on a hot Indonesian day. There are some other imported options, as Heineken and Carlsburg are quite common. Craft beers are also becoming increasingly popular in Bali. Canggu has a craft beer brewery called Black Sands. It offers great beer, but a beer here will cost more than a Bintang does. There is a craft beer place run by a Belgian man in Sanur called The Sanur Beer Garden. It actually offers decent beer at a very affordable price. Draft beers run about 30k IDR. They also offer a decent food menu. Another affordable beverage in Bali is *Arak*, the local liquor made from rice. It is absolutely awful and gives a horrific hangover. Not only that, but since it is often not regulated, the batches often can contain dangerous levels of alcohol and other harmful chemicals. In the past, people have died from drinking bad batches of *Arak*.

There are a lot of great options for going out, partying, and spending money in Bali. I have friends who go to bars where they have paid $9 USD for a Heineken. For me, I would prefer to find a small local bar or restaurant and grab a Bintang for $2 USD and hang out with like-minded friends. At the end of the day, we're drinking the same beer and enjoying good company. That is the most important thing.

Tipping

Tipping is not compulsory in Bali. In fact, a service charge is usually added to your bill. However, bear in mind that Indonesia is a developing country. Many restaurant workers earn a very modest salary. I try to be as generous as possible. Tipping is ultimately at your discretion.

Time to Eat?

Unlike Europe, you can always find restaurants open in Bali. Another plus is that they often stay open quite late. In Kuta, it's not difficult to find a place to grab a bite to eat at 11pm or midnight. Renon (in Denpasar) offers a large variety of restaurants, many of which are open quite late. If you are an early morning person, don't worry there are a few options for your 5am coffee. There are a lot of local convenience stores, Dunkin Donuts, and even McDonald's are usually open 24 hours a day. You can often find something to eat and get your morning coffee before your sunrise surf session.

CHAPTER 8: THE HONEYMOON IS OVER. – CHALLENGES TO LIVING IN BALI

Living in Bali is great, but it's not simply a life filled with coconut trees and rice paddies. Like anywhere else, there are challenges to living here. This chapter isn't meant to turn you off to living in Bali, but just to raise your awareness to the fact that there are things that aren't always easy.

Pollution

This has become an unfortunate reality in one of the most beautiful places on Earth. There are a ton of cars and motorbikes on the road in Bali, making air pollution a real problem. I often shower after a motorbike ride just to get the smoke and exhaust off of my skin. Burning rubbish only adds to the air pollution problems. Further, with many small villages throwing their rubbish into rivers that drain into the ocean, marine pollution has become a horrific problem. After China, Indonesia is the second largest marine polluter in the world. Surfing spots close to river mouths in the rainy season can be disgusting. Bali is taking steps to fight pollution. The island is currently engaged in a 'plastic detox' which includes a total ban on plastic bags and drinking straws. While these are positive steps, the problem remains apparent.

Over-Development / Over-Population

One of the reasons that the island deals with such pollution is the overdevelopment and overpopulation of the island. In fact, most of the population is concentrated in the southern part of the island. Years ago, I remember reading that Bali's population is nearly ten times what the ideal population should be for this island. As the island's economy is driven by tourism, local officials have no incentive to stop the development. More people coming to Bali = more money. So rice fields continue to be cleared to make room for luxury villas. Flooding during the rainy season is quite common in many areas as the earth has been covered with concrete and blacktop which fail to absorb the rains. There has even been talk of a Formula-1 track being built on the island.

Corruption

Many of the decisions surrounding development in Bali are not based on what's best for the island or its local people. Rather, they are based on what puts money into certain people's pockets. Corruption is rampant all throughout Indonesia – not just Bali. While the government has taken steps over the last several decades to reduce the level of corruption, it is still widespread. How well you are able to cope with living in Bali long term will be impacted by the extent to which you can accept – or at least tolerate – corruption.

Things don't always work 'as they are supposed to'. However, corruption does in fact have certain benefits. For example, you are required to have a motorbike license to ride a motorbike in Bali. If you don't have the license and are stopped at a roadblock, you should be given a ticket. The ticket usually costs around 250,000 IDR. The police will give you the ticket and take your motorbike documents. When you go to the police station and pay the ticket, you will get your documents back. This is a real inconvenience. Alternatively, you can simply pay the cop 50,000 IDR (far less than the cost of the ticket) and just continue on your way.

Another major inconvenience is filing police reports. If you lose your passport or have something stolen, you will need a police report. This should be free, and it often is. However, there are certain police stations and police officers who will create the report, but then ask for an 'administrative fee' before they can release it to you. This is not legal, but it does happen. It's usually only a few US dollars, so many people choose to simply pay it, and go about their business.

Visa extensions are another gray area where money talks. This has become more complicated over the years, as many immigration offices have signs indicating that they do not accept bribes. If you are extending a tourist or social visa and you usually have to lodge your application, and then wait for your extension to be approved. For a fee (usually around 1 million IDR), this process can be done on the same day. If you have a friend who knows someone in the immigration office, they can help you. If not, you can contact a visa agent to assist you. They are essentially paying the immigration official on your behalf. Just remember that they need to get paid, too. Similarly, if you are out of visa extensions and need to leave the country for a visa run, you can get an illegal extension. This is where an immigration officer simply stamps your passport saying you arrived back in the country from abroad. This can lead to questions when you leave the country (as there is no corresponding exit stamp). However, I know many people who've done this and none who have had a problem. Ultimately, if you want to reduce your exposure to corruption, its always best to follow the letter of the law.

Traffic

Traffic in Bali has become a huge issue. For as long as I can remember, it has always been an issue in and around Kuta. However, it has now spread out to other parts of the island. Canggu has become a digital nomad hotspot and the traffic heading out from Kuta, through Legian, Seminyak, Kerobokan, and into Canggu has been awful. Even the roads in Denpasar are very congested. There are currently plans to build a subway in Bali, but don't count on it. The plans for a subway and the existence of the toll road may help reduce traffic, but they also feed the problems associated with overdevelopment. If you want to live in any of the major tourist areas, you need to accept traffic as a way of life here.

Illness / Medical Care

Medical care has improved in Bali over the years. However, it is not comparable to Western standards. It is advisable to have evacuation insurance in the event of any serious illness. Fortunately, countries like Singapore are a short plane ride. Just bear in mind that you will have to get on a plane to get that quality of care. While there is no malaria in Bali, Dengue fever is prevalent. The biggest risk is bacteria from contaminated food and water. Over time, your body will build up immunity, but you may experience 'Bali Belly' in your first few weeks or months.

Risk of Terrorism

It is important to note this as a final thought. Bali was the site of some horrific bombings, including the attack on the Sari Club in 2002. While anti-Western sentiment exists among some people in certain parts of Indonesia, I want to stress that I have always felt safe in Bali. With the prevalence of guns and shootings in America, I feel far safer in Bali than I do at home.

CHAPTER 9: WHERE TO NOW? – LOCATIONS

Where you choose to live in Bali will have a big impact on the type of experience that you have on the island. It will also impact what you pay for your cost of living. This chapter will present some of the most common (and some relatively unheard of) locations on the island. In presenting some of the pros and cons of each place, hopefully you're able to make a more informed decision about where you choose to settle. Remember that if you choose a cheap option for accommodation (like a *kos*), you can move frequently until you find an area suited to your personal tastes.

Canggu

It's important to start here because Canggu has become one of, if not the most popular place on the island. When I lived in Canggu in 2007, I paid 5 million IDR for my apartment FOR THE ENTIRE YEAR. Those days are gone. This is one of the most expensive areas on the island. There are beautiful luxury villas, with digital nomads and influencers who spend a few hours per day working on their business in between yoga classes. If you can afford it, it's fantastic. It offers a vibrant community with great surfing, yoga, incredible food (lots of vegan/vegetarian options), bars, cafes, and pretty much anything you could hope for. It is no longer a quiet, low-key place to live.

Ubud

Ubud is the cultural and artistic center of Bali. Surrounded by lush jungles this town is often a retreat for those seeking a deeper connection with nature. Yoga studios and holistic wellness centers are everywhere, attracting travelers and long-time residents who are interested in the more spiritual side of Bali. There are ancient temples, traditional dance performances, and Balinese markets. Overall, Ubud offers a true Balinese cultural experience. Ubud is a favorite destination for those looking for a blend of art, nature, and spirituality in the center of the island. Only a few short decades ago, Ubud was largely untouched. Unfortunately, many rice fields have been cleared to build luxury villas. The center of Ubud is also not immune from the traffic jams that characterize the southern part of the island.

Kuta / Legian

Kuta is often the first port of call for travelers to Bali, as it is very close to the airport. It has beautiful golden beaches, which are unfortunately often covered in trash. It has a lively energy and is a magnet for partygoers. While there are tons of surfers all along the beach, there are undoubtedly higher-quality waves throughout the rest of the island. Kuta is the epicenter of Bali's nightlife, and it transforms after sunset, offering a ton of bars, clubs, and beach parties. The streets are lined with shops, restaurants, and street vendors, all of whom are anxious to sell you things. Beyond the nightlife, Kuta also provides shopping like Beachwalk Mall. It's a good choice for those who want to be close to the beach, but also need a very active social scene.

Bukit

Positioned high up on the cliffs of Bali's southern peninsula, the Bukit offers amazing views of the Indian Ocean. This is the center of Indonesian surfing, with world-class breaks like Uluwatu and Padang Padang. The Bukit has beautiful beaches, luxurious resorts, and stunning cliff-top villas. All of this comes with a price tag attached to it. The laid-back atmosphere complements the upscale amenities, making it an ideal choice for those who want luxury, tranquility, great beaches and waves, and can afford to pay for it all. Check out Suluban Beach's hidden caves and Bingin Beach.

Seminyak

Seminyak shows Bali's more sophisticated side. It combines upscale living, eating, and shopping with a coastal vibe. It is famous for its stylish beach clubs, boutique shopping, and gourmet dining. Seminyak may be the place for you if you are seeking luxury in Bali. Even if you don't live in The Yak, it is a great place to visit. There are tons of trendy boutiques and designer stores, offering a great shopping experience. Sunset cocktails at beach clubs like Ku De Ta make for incredible evenings. Luxury villas and resorts with private pools provide an exclusive setting for those wanting to indulge in Bali's high-end lifestyle.

Kerobokan

Situated between the popular areas of Seminyak and Canggu, Kerobokan is a peaceful 'neighborhood' location that is still close to many popular spots on the island. It is far more affordable than either Canggu or Seminyak. It is a residential area that provides a peaceful neighborhood while being within reach of the more vibrant scenes nearby. The area features a mix of traditional markets, local eateries, and contemporary establishments, catering to a diverse range of tastes. Kerobokan's strategic location appeals to those who are looking for an affordable and calm environment without sacrificing access to the busier and more popular areas of the island. It also offers many of the same amenities found in neighboring areas.

Nusa Dua

Nusa Dua is another one of Bali's luxurious areas. Property here has really sky-rocketed in value. I once spent the rainy season renting a villa in Nusa and it was incredible. However, many of those same villas now have huge price tags attached to them. It is famous for its white-sand beaches and high-end resorts. The area's manicured gardens, upscale spas, and golf courses create a more exclusive, upper-class ambiance. There are still areas where you can find more peaceful, local-style living. At this point, anything on the beach is pricey. Nusa Dua's Geger Beach is very popular surf spot in the rainy season with huge waves breaking far off the coast.

Sanur

Sanur is one of my favorite spots in Bali. It is a charming little town with a really laid-back atmosphere and incredible beaches. It was formerly popular as a retirement community for expats, but it has now grown to be popular with expats of all ages. Sleepier than other areas on the other side of the island, it is known for its calm waters and coral reefs. The coastline is lined with traditional fishing boats, and the paved beachfront promenade is perfect for morning jogs. There are even free yoga classes on the beach at sunrise (in Indonesian). Sanur's local markets and beachfront cafes offer a taste of authentic Balinese life. The beach side of the by-pass is more expensive, but if you are willing to live on the opposite side (closer to Renon), you can still find some bargains.

Denpasar

Denpasar is the capital of the island and is a melting pot of culture, commerce, and history. It is also probably the part of the island where you will find the best bargains. Denpasar hosts important government offices, markets, and cultural institutions. The Badung Market is an incredible early morning shopping experience, offering everything from fresh produce to traditional crafts. Historic sites like the Bajra Sandhi Monument and Puputan Square are great spots to visit if you are interested in Bali's cultural heritage. Denpasar's central location makes it easy to explore the rest of the island. I have lived in Denpasar for several years and it really combines the conveniences of city life with access to the rest of Bali's attractions... and it's cheap.

Renon

Renon, situated within Denpasar, offers a peaceful residential escape amidst the energy of the city. This district is known for its spacious parks, government offices, and cultural landmarks. The lush Bajra Sandhi Monument Park provides a beautiful area for residents to walk, jog, or ride bicycles. There are many nearby government buildings, so you may need to visit Renon for visa extensions if that is the area of the island you call home. Renon offers a more relaxed pace compared to the rest of Denpasar, making it a great choice for those seeking a quiet and green environment within the urban landscape. With its blend of modern conveniences and green spaces, Renon provides a unique and balanced living experience in Bali.

Tabanan

Tabanan, in the western part of the island, was once considered an out of the way destination. However, as development moves north of Canggu, this has become a choice for many foreign residents. It offers an escape into rural beauty. Surrounded by terraced rice fields, lush rainforests, and sacred temples, Tabanan showcases the island's natural and cultural richness. The Jatiluwih Rice Terraces are recognized by UNESCO for their incredible beauty. Tanah Lot Temple perched on a sea rock provides a spiritual allure. Tabanan allows for a peaceful lifestyle away from the tourist hubs and offers a genuine Balinese experience. Those seeking a retreat into nature and cultural authenticity will find Tabanan to be a hidden gem.

Ketewel

Ketewel is a small village on Bali's eastern coast. It is a very traditional Balinese neighborhood and offers an escape from the island's busier tourist areas. Known for its black sand beaches and traditional fishing communities, Ketewel really shows the authentic coastal lifestyle. While it is largely home to locals, there have been luxury villas popping up all over the place on the east side of the island. Ketewel is a great spot for those who appreciate the quieter and more traditional side of Bali, away from the hustle and bustle of the popular tourist destinations.

Candidasa

Candidasa is a bit further away from the airport. It is a real gem on Bali's east coast. Since it is so far removed from the area of Kuta / Legian, it is popular for those seeking a slower pace of life. The area is renowned for its coral-rich waters, making it a favorite among snorkelers and divers. The laid-back ambiance is complemented by beachfront resorts and traditional Balinese architecture. Candidasa is a haven for those who appreciate coastal charm, cultural authenticity, and the opportunity to explore the underwater wonders of Bali's eastern shores.

Medewi

Medewi is far up the west coast of Bali, very close to where you can hop the ferry to Java. It is really a hidden paradise on Bali's west coast. It offers a long left-hand surf break and is popular among surfers seeking a more secluded experience. The area is a mix of Balinese and Javanese residents. Medewi's black sand beaches and gentle waves create a picturesque setting for those looking to escape the crowds and experience nature. While popular for surfing, Medewi also offers a great escape for those people who want a more laid-back and off-the-beaten-path Bali experience.

Singaraja

As Bali's former capital, Singaraja on the island's northern coast holds a lot of cultural and historical significance. The town exhibits colonial architecture, traditional markets, and remnants of its Dutch colonial past. The Gedong Kirtya Historical Library and the Royal Palace of Singaraja are great places to visit to learn about the town's heritage. Singaraja is also a great place to visit for the waterfalls and mountainous landscapes of northern Bali.

While very far from the south, Singaraja is a place that you should at the very least make a visit to while you are living in Bali. If you don't mind being away from it all, you may choose to call this place home.

Lovina

Northen Bali has always been an amazingly beautiful place. This area of the island really grew in popularity after the 2002 bombings in Kuta. Many Westerners wanted to avoid the popular tourist sites of southern Bali, so they started to make their way northward. Lovina is renowned for its black sand beaches and dolphin-filled waters. Many people who live on the other side of the island come to Lovina to swim with the dolphins. The laid-back atmosphere and scenic landscapes make Lovina an ideal destination for a peaceful weekend retreat. Early morning boat rides offer the chance to witness playful dolphins in their natural habitat. While not a spot for surfing, Lovina's calm seas are a great place for swimming and snorkeling, away from the busier southern regions of Bali. The coastal village has everything from beachfront resorts, local markets, and authentic warungs. It provides a genuine experience for those looking to unwind in a more secluded and authentic Bali setting.

CHAPTER 10: SAY WHAT? – SURVIVAL INDONESIAN

Hello – *halo*

How are you? – *Apa Kabar?*

I'm fine. – *Baik*

What's your name? – *Siapa nama (kamu)*

Where are you from? – *Kamu dari mana?*

How much is this? – *Berapa harga ini?*

This / That – *Ini / Itu*

My name is Jay. – *Nama saya Jay.*

I am from America. – *Saya dari Amerika.*

Are you married? – *Sudah kawin? / Sudah menika?*

Do you have a family? – *Sudah punya keluarga?*

How long have you been here? – *Berapa lama di sini?*

Can you speak Indonesian? – *Bisa Bahasa Indonesia?*

Please – *silahkan*

Thank you – *terima kasih*

You are welcome – *sama sama*

Excuse me – *permisi*

Good morning – *selamat pagi*

Good afternoon – *selamat siang*

Good afternoon / evening – *selamat sore*

Good night – *selamat malam*

Welcome – *selamat datang*

Goodbye – *selamat jalan* (others are leaving)

Goodbye – *selamat tinggal* (you are leaving)

Sorry – *ma'af*

I – *saya* (formal) *aku* (informal)

You – anda (formal) kamu (informal)

We – kita (inclusive) kami (exclusive)

He / She – dia

They - *Mereka*

To have – *ada / punya*

To want – *mau / ingin*

To be able to – *bisa*

To eat – *makan*

To drink – *minum*

Food – *makanan*

Drink / Beverage – *minuman*

Rice – *nasi*

Noodles – *mie*

Chicken – *ayam*

Goat – *kambing*

Fish – *ikan*

Beef – *sapi (daging sapi)*

Tofu – *tahu*

Pig – *babi (babi guling* = Balinese suckling pig)

Apple – *apel*

Banana – *pisang*

Bread - *roti*

Water – *air*

Juice – *jus*

Beer – *bir*

Coffee – *kopi*

Tea – *teh*

Milk - *susu*

Hot – *panas*

Cold – *dingin*

Ice - *es*

Already – sudah

Not yet – *belum*

With – *dengan / sama*

Here – *di sini*

There – *di sana*

To – *ke*

And – *dan*

Number (Nomor)

One – Satu

Two – Dua

Three – Tiga

Four – Empat

Five – Lima

Six – Enam

Seven – Tujuh

Eight – Delapan

Nine – Sembilan

Ten - Sepuluh

Also by James J. Riley, EdS

Moving to Portugal: How I immigrated to Portugal and how you can too!

Teaching English Online: Leave Home, Live Rich, Retire Early- A How-To Guide for Digital Nomads

Think Success: Fifteen Rules for Establishing and Maintaining a Successful Mindset

Speak Easy: An English Language Activity Book- Beginner Level

From Sentence to Essay: Using Cartoon Characters to Develop Descriptive Writing with Young Learners

Author Bio

James "Jay" Riley is originally from Long Island, New York. He has been an educator for nearly twenty years and a world traveler his entire life. He holds MBA, MAcc, MA TESOL, and EdS degrees. He has lived, worked, and traveled all over the world, but currently splits his time between Indonesia, Spain, and Portugal.

---

[1] https://www.embassyofindonesia.org/basic-facts/
[2] https://data.worldbank.org/country/ID
[3] https://www.worldometers.info/demographics/indonesia-demographics/
[4] https://data.worldbank.org/indicator/SE.ADT.LITR.ZS?end=2018&locations=ID&start=1980
[5] https://wenr.wes.org/2019/03/education-in-indonesia-2

Printed in Great Britain
by Amazon